I Go

by Peter Bardetti   illustrated by Pam Thomson

SCHOOL PUBLISHERS

Copyright © by Harcourt, Inc.

All rights reserved. No part of this publication may be reproduced or transmitted in any form or by any means, electronic or mechanical, including photocopy, recording, or any information storage and retrieval system, without permission in writing from the publisher.

Requests for permission to make copies of any part of the work should be addressed to School Permissions and Copyrights, Harcourt, Inc., 6277 Sea Harbor Drive, Orlando, Florida 32887-6777. Fax: 407-345-2418.

HARCOURT and the Harcourt Logo are trademarks of Harcourt, Inc., registered in the United States of America and/or other jurisdictions. Printed in China

ISBN 10 0-15-364045-6
ISBN 13 978-0-15-364045-2

8 9 10   0940   17 16 15 14 13 12 11 10

Ordering Options
ISBN 10 0-15-364145-2
ISBN 13 978-0-15-364145-9

Cars go.

 Trucks go.

 Buses go.

Trains go.

Boats go.

 Planes go.

I go!

I Go
Word Count: 16

High-Frequency Words
go

I